A MATTER *of the* HEART

For where your treasure is, there your heart will be also. Matthew 6: 21

MIKE MCCORMICK WITH JOANN NASER

WESTBOW®
PRESS
A DIVISION OF THOMAS NELSON
& ZONDERVAN

WestBow Press books may be ordered through booksellers or by contacting:

WestBow Press
A Division of Thomas Nelson & Zondervan
1663 Liberty Drive
Bloomington, IN 47403
www.westbowpress.com
1 (866) 928-1240

ISBN: 978-1-4908-7325-1 (sc)
ISBN: 978-1-4908-7327-5 (hc)
ISBN: 978-1-4908-7326-8 (e)

Library of Congress Control Number: 2015904150

Print information available on the last page.

WestBow Press rev. date: 03/16/2015

Contents

PREFACE

One major decision Christians face is how much they give to churches and to charities that glorify God.

Many Christians are guided by either a poverty mentality or a prosperity mentality when it comes to money. I submit that both positions are removed from the teachings of the Scripture.

The poverty mentality holds that a true Christian life lies in deprivation and self-denial. Yet Scripture teachings suggest otherwise. God wants us to have an enjoyable life on this Earth so we can provide both for our loved ones and ourselves.

Work is a part of God's creation, so when we work and provide work for others, we are serving God.

The parable of the talent demonstrates that God wants us to invest wisely. The third person in the talent buries his money in the ground, and is admonished for doing so. He is told not to give the money to the poor, but to the first person who invests wisely.

The prosperity mentality, in contrast, holds that "God wants you to be rich." While God wants us to prosper, the Scripture categorically rejects wealth used to gratify our own ego and selfish desires. We should not use our wealth merely for self-promotion and to make us look good.

I spent a lot of my life applying prosperity thinking to my businesses, thinking about what I was going to accomplish or make happen in this world. I believe the phrase, "if it is to be, it's up to me."[1] There is no ill will in that statement or in similar affirmations based on positive thinking.

But as I grew older, I realized after many trials and tribulations, that my fate was not up to me, but it was up to God. Any gains I made applying prosperity thinking were merely self-serving and temporary.

It must be pointed out that our material conditions are the central focus of both philosophies. Whether you have a lot or a little, it is based on the stuff you have.

Stewardship, in contrast, puts God and being a disciple for Jesus Christ at the center of the attention. All those things that we create are to serve Him. Our words, attitudes, condition of our heart, and how we handle our money, that is all how we bring glory to God.

I have written previously about how people can learn to invest properly and to live within their means.[2] But giving is the critical ingredient in being a true Christian.

---

[1] Johnsen, William H. "Self-Reliance." Quotationbooks.com.

[2] McCormick, Mike. My Life Matters: Finding and Funding your God-given Purpose. Xulon Press, Longwood, FL. 2008

Jesus told his followers that to be his disciple, you have to give up everything. Not only does God own everything, but also we have to be good managers with a joyful heart. We will stand before God, and be held accountable for how we used our blessings.

I was created **by** God, I was created **like** God, but most importantly, and it took me a while to fully realize this, I was created **for** God. God provides resources to honor or glorify Him. Having resources is a great blessing, but a great responsibility as well.

Whether you have a lot or a little, we all face the pull of a culture that devalues those things that are truly important. The Scriptures consider those who give in to the pull of the money culture as foolish, because they glorify themselves over God.

Sacrificial Giving

People spend more time planning their vacations or retirements than they do for eternity. These priorities need to change. Our responsibility transcends our own lives.

> Money is not an end, but the means to glorifying God.

It is all used for His glory. It is not enslaving, but empowering. God provides resources to those who seek to glorify Him. Our wealth should be used to help others and tell people around the world about Jesus Christ who have yet to hear about Him.

It is no different to having a solid investment portfolio than to have a productive philanthropic plan. Both requires diligence, hard work, and a long-term vision and sticking to it.

Most importantly, philanthropy should occur through the eternal perspective. It does not work well with individuals who do not have an eternal perspective.

How much should we give? God requires different things for different people. If you are raising children, or if you have an empty nest, God would have different expectations for what you should give.

Paul implores the Corinthians to give based on one's income. The concept of tithing is based on 10 percent of our income, and is the standard benchmark. In the Old Testament, it is based on a percentage, which amounts to 23-30 percent of income. The New Testament goes even further by transcending percentages, and states that we give when God implores us to give.

No matter what percentage we decide to share in the spirit of Christ, God is looking for an obedient will, joyful attitude, and compassionate heart.

Whether we give a little bit, or everything we have, it must be done freely and gladly.

Stewardship transcends our own lives. Remember, a Christian steward is a person who is entrusted with a life redeemed by Christ. Turning everything over to God makes this stewardship possible.

Speaking of stewardship, I would like to thank Greg Devore and Bill Harmon for their editorial review of this book. It is most appreciated. Thanks go to Mike Rollage, Dave Stombaugh and Peter Fleming for their contribution to this book. Also, I would like to thank Joann Naser for her dedication and help in writing this book. You made the work easier. Special thanks to my wife, Cathie, for her support and love over many years and our children, Michael, Allison and Mark. More about them later.

All proceeds from the sale of this book will be donated to:

The Endurance Foundation
C/O The Bible Chapel
300 Gallery Drive
McMurray, PA 15317

The Scriptures used in this book are New International Version, Zondervan, Grand Rapids, MI, 2001, unless otherwise indicated.

Introduction

To write a book is an exciting endeavor! Take this journey with me and discover the joys of giving. Yes, I said joy! Even The Pittsburgh Post-Gazette agrees with me. In an editorial on October 9, 2014, it uses information from the Chronicle of Philanthropy, an authority on the nonprofit world, that "the economy (is) improving, some more cheerful giving is in order."

"Each man should give what he has decided in his heart to give, not reluctantly or under compulsion, for *God loves a cheerful giver (2 Corinthians 9:7)*."

Throughout this book, I will focus on the top 10 giving reasons. They are listed here for your convenience, but will be interspersed throughout the book. Look for them over and over again. They are some guidelines for becoming a more generous giver.

1. God wants us to remember the story of Cain and Abel (Genesis 4: 3-7).

2. God blesses us because of who He is not who we are or what we have done (2 Corinthians 8: 7-9).

3. God blesses us to bless others (Ephesians 2:10, Acts 17: 26, Esther 4: 14).

4. God blesses us to fund the Great Commission (2 Corinthians 9: 10-11, Proverbs 28: 27, Romans 10: 13-15).

5. God wants our gifts first, the best, from the heart (Proverbs 3: 9-10, Genesis 4: 3, Malachi 3: 8-12).

6. God wants us to be generous not an act, but a response. Generous giving includes an obedient will, a joyful attitude and a compassionate heart (Matthew 10: 8).

7. God wants our heart because money follows our heart (Matthew 6:21).

8. God's purposes should be our highest priority (1 Corinthians 16: 1-4).

9. God wants us to be godly and content (1 Timothy 6: 6).

10. God wants us to know that salvation is free, ministry has a cost, and there is a cost to being a disciple (Luke 14:33).

CAIN AND ABEL

In the course of time Cain brought some of the fruits of the soil as an offering to the Lord. But Abel brought fat portions from some of the firstborn of his flock. The Lord looked with favor on Abel and his offering but on Cain and his offering he did not look with favor. So Cain was very angry, and his face was downcast. Then the Lord said to Cain, "Why are you angry? Why is your face downcast? If you do what is right, will you not be accepted? But if you do not do what is right, sin is crouching at your door; it desires to have you, but you must master it."

Genesis 4: 3-7

Cain and Abel provide a chilling yet accurate story about giving. Cain gave "in the course of time" as verse three suggests, but really it was not accepted by God. He did not have a generous heart or attitude. It was not the first fruits of the land or the choicest fruits.

Abel brought "fat portions from some of the firstborn of his flock (verse four)." He sacrificed sacrificed part of his livelihood as an offering to God. He gave according to God's instruction.

> God does not separate the gift from the giver.

The Lord found favor with Abel and his generous offering. God does not separate the gift from the giver. He either approves or disapproves of it. One Webster's dictionary definition describes favor as preference for one person over another, approval or support. Don't we want God's favor in our life? We must do what is right.

"By faith Abel offered God a better sacrifice than Cain did," says Hebrews 11: 4. "By faith he was commended as a righteous man, when God spoke well of his offerings. And by faith he still speaks, even though he is dead."

Remember, God gave first. In the familiar Scripture passage, John 3:16, Jesus says, "For God so loved the world that *He gave* his one and only Son, that whoever believes in Him shall not perish but have eternal life." Salvation is the awesome and ultimate gift of God.

Cain's gift was not favored by the Lord. He found his heart to be calloused and full of jealousy. Cain, the first born son of Adam and Eve, responds in anger—not repentance. When God reveals something for us to do, we should accept it, not get angry about it! 1 John 3: 12 states, "Do not be like Cain, who belonged to the evil one and murdered his brother. And why did he murder him? Because his own actions were evil and his brother's were righteous."

God wants us to be generous, not an act, but a response to His first gifts to us. Some generous gifts include an obedient will, a joyful attitude and a compassionate heart. As Matthew 10:8 states, "Heal the sick, raise the dead, cleanse those who have leprosy, drive out demons. Freely you have received, freely give."

Cain, however, had sin crouching at his door because he was unable to give and was jealous of his brother. He made a choice—he chose sin and it mastered him.

Abel, on the other hand, had a tender and joyful heart. He freely gave an offering to the Lord which was accepted in His sight. "Honor the Lord with your wealth, with the first fruits of all your crops; then your barns will be filled to overflowing, and your vats will brim over with new wine (Proverbs 3: 9-10)."

Abel honored the Lord with his first fruits. God wants the same for us today. He does not want us to be mastered by money or things. Sin can quickly overtake you and your judgments get compromised.

> Cain was unable to trust God.

You can only have one master. Choose well today.

Joshua 24: 14, 15, "Now fear the Lord and serve Him with all faithfulness. Throw away the gods of your forefathers worshipped beyond the River and in Egypt, and serve the Lord. But if serving the Lord seems undesirable to you, then choose for yourselves this day whom you will serve, whether the gods of your forefathers served beyond the River, or the gods of the Amorites, in whose land you are living. But as for me and my household, we will serve the Lord."

Paul, in 2 Corinthians 8: 7 states, "But just as you excel in everything—in faith, in speech, in knowledge, in complete earnestness and in your love for us—see that you also excel in this grace of giving."

You want to excel in so many things, why not giving? Jesus was the perfect example. Before His crucifixion, He washed the disciples' feet and gave thanks for being the broken bread and the poured-out wine.

The Doctrine of God	
a. God is One	Exodus 15: 11, Deut. 4: 35, Psalm 86: 10
b. God is Compassionate	Psalm 86: 15, 145: 8, 2 Cor. 1: 3
c. God is Eternal	Deut. 33: 27, Lam. 5: 19
d. God is Faithful, Trustworthy	2 Sam. 7: 28, Psalm 33: 4
e. God is Good	Psalm 31: 19, 34: 8, 52: 9, 73: 1
f. God is Gracious	Psalm 86: 15, 111: 4, 145: 9
g. God is Holy	Isaiah 6: 3
h. God is Impartial	Romans 2: 6
i. God is Just	Psalm 97: 2
j. God is Love	Psalm 136: 1
k. God is Merciful	Hebrews 4: 16
l. God is Omnipotent	Job 42: 2
m. God is Omnipresent	Psalm 139: 8
n. God is Omniscient	Psalm 139: 4

o.	God is Patient, Longsuffering, Forbearing	Psalm 78: 38
p.	God is Righteous	Psalm 119: 137
q.	God is Self-Existent	John 5: 26
r.	God is Truthful	Psalm 33: 4
s.	God is Unchangeable	Psalm 33: 11
t.	God possess Freedom (Sovereignty)	Psalm 24: 1
u.	God shows Loving Kindness	Psalm 18: 50

Ann Voskamp, in her New York Times best-selling book, One Thousand Gifts Devotional: Reflections on Finding Everyday Graces, speaks of eucharisteo. It is a Greek word "that expresses what Christ did at the Last Supper: take the bread of pain as grace," explains Voskamp. "Give thanks for that which is hard. Endure the cross, all in view of the joy set before."[3]

"Therefore, since we are surrounded by such a great cloud of witnesses, let us throw off everything that hinders and the sin that so easily entangles, and let us run with perseverance the race marked out for us. Let us fix our eyes on Jesus, the author and perfecter of our faith, who

---

[3] Voskamp, Ann. One Thousand Gifts Devotional: Reflections on Finding Everyday Graces. Zondervan, Ann Arbor, MI, 2012. P, 188.

for the joy set before Him endured the cross, scorning its shame, and sat down at the right hand of the throne of God. Consider Him who endured such opposition from sinful men, so that you will not grow weary and lose heart (Hebrews 12: 1-3)."

It may be hard for you to be generous, counter-intuitive but believe me, it is worth it. Remember, that in giving away is the receiving of joy. God wants us to remember the lessons from the story of Cain and Abel (Genesis 4: 3-7).

> God blesses us because of who He is. Not because of what we do.

DIVIDED HEARTS

*Do not store up for yourselves treasure on
earth, where moth and rust destroy, and
where thieves break in and steal. But store
up for yourselves treasures in heaven, where
moth and rust do not destroy, and where
thieves do not break in and steal. For where
your treasure is, there your heart will be
also.*

Matthew 6: 19-21

I am more like Cain than I would like to admit. Sometimes I would like to take the easy way out and not give something of true value. Chip Ingram wrote, "I recently cleaned out my garage, put everything I didn't want into plastic bags, and made a run to Goodwill. I unloaded it, got a receipt that would allow me to write it off on my taxes, and went back home. What I did in cleaning up and getting a tax write-off was wise, but it wasn't generous. I did not want any of that stuff. Generosity is about giving from your heart, and a heartfelt gift is a high priority and of high quality."[4]

Cain gave out of a divided heart of what he wanted to give and when he wanted to give. It was unacceptable to God. There are seven other examples in the Bible that I would like to focus on because of their divided hearts. They were unable to fulfill their mission with God although sometimes they did change. Somebody said there are only two kinds of people in the world. There are those who wake up in the morning and say, "Good morning, Lord" and there are those who wake up and say, "Good Lord, it's morning." These seven may be examples of the latter.

1. Jonah

Poor Jonah. He doesn't listen to God and he is challenged by his decision. The word of the Lord came to Jonah, "Go to the great city of Nineveh and preach against it because its wickedness has come up before Me," states Jonah 1: 2.

This is an example in Scripture that God not only cared for the Jewish people, but others as well. Nineveh was the capital of the vast and powerful Assyrian empire. Instead of

> Independence +
> Disobedience =
> Recipe for Disaster
> (See Deuteronomy 28)

---

[4]   Ingram, Chip. The Genius of Generosity. Generous Church, Los Gatos, CA. P. 40.

traveling to Nineveh, Jonah travels to Tarshish, thinking he would escape from God.

The ship sets sail and soon after a storm breaks out. The seamen pray to their own gods and cast lots to see who is causing this trouble. The lot fell, of course, to Jonah. He realized that he was the cause for the storm and asked to be thrown overboard. Not wanting to harm him, they tried to row back to land. They were unable to do it. They threw Jonah overboard and the sea calmed. "At this the men greatly feared the Lord, and they offered a sacrifice to the Lord and made vows to Him," states Jonah 1: 16. Using Jonah's disobedience, God reveals Himself to sailors.

God provided a great fish to swallow Jonah. Some scholars believe it was a whale. God can use anything to get your attention. Can you imagine being inside a whale? Jonah prayed and "the Lord commanded the fish, and it vomited Jonah onto dry land," says Jonah 2: 10.

Can you imagine what Jonah would look like after being in a whale's stomach for three days? No wonder the people of Nineveh listened to him. He finally obeyed God and preached in the city of Nineveh. Jonah prophesied, "Forty more days and Nineveh would be overturned," in Jonah 3: 4.

An amazing thing happened. The Ninevites believed God. They declared a fast and put on sackcloth, a symbol of mourning. When God saw that they turned from their wicked ways, He had compassion on them and did not plan to destroy them.

Instead of rejoicing at the graciousness of God, Jonah takes a temper tantrum. He was mad that God spared these 120,000 people. He wanted to die. God spared his life, but at the end of the book, it does not show Jonah remorseful for his actions. He wanted things his own way.

2. Samson

Samson was announced by an angel to his parents, but unfortunately, this man lived a carnal lifestyle for many years. He was a charismatic figure—physically very powerful but he had a weakness for immoral women. He was not to cut his hair, which was the source of his power, or drink wine.

The best known story about Samson is his desire for Delilah. She eventually wore him down to tell her about his hair and he ends up blind and weak. God appointed him judge over Israel, but he ends up in a Philistine prison. Samson prays, "O Sovereign Lord, remember me, O God, please strengthen me just once more, and let me with one blow get revenge on the Philistines for my two eyes," Judges 16: 28.

Samson was to perform before the Philistines, but he asked God for strength to pull down the central pillars in the temple (Judges 16: 29-30). Samson dies along with many Philistines. Think about how Samson's story could have been different if he had obeyed God and sought Him more and his heart was not divided.

3. Gomer

"When the word of the Lord began to speak through Hosea," the Lord said to him, "'go take yourself an adulterous wife and children of unfaithfulness, because the land is guilty of the vilest adultery in departing from the Lord,'" Hosea 1: 2.

Hosea marries Gomer and they have a son together named Jezreel. She goes on to have a daughter named Lo-Ruhamah, which means not loved. Can you imagine naming your child that name? It does not specifically state that the daughter was Hosea's like the son. The Scripture reads "children of unfaithfulness."

Gomer also had a son, Lo-Ammi, which means "you are not my people, and I am not your God (Hosea 1: 9)." Then Gomer leaves Hosea for other adulterous relationships. "The Lord said to me, 'Go, show your love to your wife again, though she is loved by another and is an adulteress. Love her as the Lord loves the Israelites, though they turn to other gods (Hosea 3: 1).'"

So Hosea buys back his wife for 15 shekels (6 ounces) of silver and about 10 bushels of barley. He tells her to live with him for many days that she should not be a prostitute again. We do not hear from Gomer in Hosea. We do not know if she changed her ways. Let us not be stubborn in our paths, but choose God.

The story appears to be an analogy for the Lord's forgiveness to a wayward Israel, which He promised to "betroth you to Me forever, I will betroth you in righteousness and justice, in love and compassion. I will betroth you in faithfulness, and you will acknowledge the Lord," states Hosea 2: 19-20.

God is waiting for us to seek Him—let us not turn our backs on Him like Gomer.

4. Judas Iscariot

Judas was selected as one of the 12 disciples of Jesus. He walked with Him for three years. He had an important role as treasurer for the group although he was dishonest. When Mary anointed Jesus' feet with an expensive perfume, Judas became indignant. "Why wasn't this perfume sold and the money given to the poor? It was worth a year's wages. He did not say this because he cared about the poor but because he was a thief; as keeper of the money bag, he used to help himself to what was put in it (John 12: 5-6)."

Jesus rebuked him by stating, "Leave her alone ... It was intended that she should save this perfume for the day of my burial. You will always have the poor among you, but you will not always have Me (John 12: 7-8)."

Judas soon after began plotting to betray Jesus. Judas entered a black hole, which he could not escape. He didn't want to. "Then one of the 12-the one called Judas Iscariot—went to the chief priests and asked, 'What are you willing to give me if I had Him over to you?' So they counted out for him 30 silver coins. From then on Judas watched for an opportunity to hand Him over (Matthew 26: 14-15)."

After the Lord's Supper, Judas gathers a large crowd armed with swords and clubs sent from the chief priests, away from the Passover crowds. The betrayer arranged a signal: "The one I kiss is the Man; arrest Him. Going at once to Jesus, Judas said, 'Greetings, Rabbi!' and kissed Him (Matthew 26: 48-49)."

Jesus knew what Judas had in his heart but He did not send him away. Jesus gave him the opportunity to choose, but Judas already had made his choice. Luke 22: 3 states that Satan entered Judas.

After Judas learned that Jesus was condemned to be crucified, "he was seized with remorse and returned the 30 silver coins to the chief priests and the elders. 'I have sinned,' he said, 'for I have betrayed innocent blood.' 'What is that to us?' they replied. 'That's your responsibility.' So Judas threw the money into the temple and left. Then he went away and hanged himself (Matthew 27: 3-5)."

The chief priests decided to purchase a potter's field to bury foreigners since they decided it could not be placed in the treasury again. "That is why it has been called the Field of Blood to this day. Then what was spoken by Jeremiah the prophet was fulfilled: 'They took 30 silver coins, the price set on Him by the people of Israel, and they used them to by the potter's field, as the Lord commanded me (Matthew 27: 9-10)."

The Bible does state that Judas had remorse, but it did not say that he repented. Let us be careful about our actions. We do not want to fall into a black hole of sin that we cannot escape.

5. *Ananias and Sapphira*

The book of Acts talks about the new believers and how they shared with everyone. "Barnabas (which means Son of Encouragement), sold a field he owned and brought the money and put it at the apostles' feet," says Acts 4: 36.

Ananias and Sapphira also sold a property. However, with his wife's knowledge, Ananias kept back a portion of the money for himself. He brought the rest and put it at the apostles' feet. Then Peter said, "Ananias, how is that Satan has so filled your heart that you have lied to the Holy Spirit and have kept for yourself some of the money you received from the land? Didn't it belong to you before it was sold? And after it was sold, wasn't the money at your disposal? What made you think of doing such a thing? You have not lied to men but to God. When Ananias heard this, he fell down and died (Acts 5: 3-5)."

This caused some fear in the people. A few hours later, his wife, Sapphira, came to the temple. Peter asked her the price of the land. She agreed with the amount that Ananias had gave. Peter said to her: "How could you agree to test the Spirit of the Lord (Acts 5: 9)?"

It certainly was not worth the price Ananias and Sapphira paid for lying over their gift to God. He knows and will judge us on all things! Let us give willingly and wholeheartedly.

6. Lot's Wife

Lot is an interesting Scriptural character. Abraham's nephew, Lot chose the land that looked fertile and left the other land for his uncle. Their herdsmen had disputes because they were both so wealthy and could not share one land (Genesis 13). Lot ends up in Sodom. One evening, he greets two angels who stay in his home. The evil men of the city gather outside his home and tell him to let out the two men so they can have sex (Genesis 19). Lot tells them to not do such a wicked thing but he would give the crowd his two virgin daughters, who were engaged to other men.

The men from the inside reached out to bring Lot back into the house. In the night, the angels take them out of the city. "Flee for your lives! Flee to the mountains or you will be swept away (Genesis 19: 17)."

The Lord rained down burning sulfur on Sodom and Gomorrah. But Lot's wife, no other name given, did not obey the angels and she looked back and became a pillar of salt (Genesis 19: 25).

Sometimes aren't we tempted to look back? It cost Lot's wife her life. Don't get caught up in past mistakes or choices. Keep moving forward with the Lord. Otherwise, it could be very costly.

7. The Rich Young Ruler

Jesus meets a rich young ruler and begins a great example. First the ruler asks what he must do to inherit eternal life. Jesus tells him to obey the commandments. He answers he has kept them since he was a child.

"Jesus looked at him and loved him, 'One thing you lack,' he said in Mark 10: 21. 'Go and sell everything you have and give to the poor, and you will have treasure in heaven. Then come, follow Me.'"

- He had no desire to help the poor.
- He had no love for his neighbors.
- He was self-indulgent and selfish.
- He had the sins of omission and commission.
- He wanted an easy future without godly influence.

At this, the man went away sad. Jesus told His disciples how hard it is for a rich man to enter heaven. They asked then who could be saved? "With man this is impossible, but not with God; all things are possible with God (Mark 10: 27)."

Every day we make choices that can affect our spiritual growth and development. Let us always try and focus on what God wants and not what we want or have.

Where your treasure is, there your heart will be also. Matthew 6: 21 Randy Alcorn in his book, The Treasure Principle, states that the Scripture is his second principle.

Towards the end of the book, we will look at transformed hearts. Remember, God blesses us to bless others (Ephesians 2: 10). Randy Alcorn states, God "doesn't bless us to raise a standard of living, he blesses us to raise our standard of giving."[5]

---

[5] Alcorn, Randy. <u>The Treasure Principle</u>. Multnomah Books, New York, NY, 2001. P. 75.

ANGERED HEART
REFLECTED ON HIS FACE

The Lord looked with favor on Abel and his offering, but on Cain and his offering he did not look with favor. So Cain was very angry, and his face was downcast. Then the Lord said to Cain, "Why are you angry? Why is your face downcast? If you do what is right, will you not be accepted? But if you do not do what is right, sin is crouching at your door; it desires to have you, but you must master it.

Genesis 4: 4-7

Several years ago, I was invited to speak to the group Mothers of Preschoolers (MOPS). The group was studying God's Word through understanding His universe. I decided to relate financial issues to black holes.

To begin the session, I asked three rhetorical questions:

1. Is it true that what goes up must come down?
2. Is it true that practice makes perfect?
3. Is it true that time flies when you are having fun?

The truth about question one is answered by the space program. Frequently, things are launched into space, rockets or satellites, which are not meant to come down. They have escaped the gravitational pull and will not come down to earth.

Only perfect practice makes perfect. I can tell by my golf game that practice does not make perfect. I continue to make improper swings and make casual attempts to improve. In 1976 at the summer Olympics, Nadia Comaneci score a perfect 10 during her gymnastics routine on the uneven parallel bars. It was the first time in history for a perfect score in gymnastics. Her practice was perfect.

Time flies when you are having fun? It really does not. If you are in a black hole, time is distorted. Someone with sin or financial problems may feel that time is moving very slowly.

There can be a point of no return if you are lingering near a black hole. Remember, the black hole does not pull you in. But it could be one more act whether it is gambling, pornography, addictions, or mismanagement of money that can send you into the black hole which you cannot escape.

> There is a saying that if you do not master sin, it will master you as God speaks to Cain about it in Genesis 4.

James also talks about God does not judge what is the external but what is on the inside of us that leads to sin.

Drinking, pornography, gambling, greed, desire to get rich quick, overspending, poor stewardship, mismanagement of funds and not understanding money, can lead you further and further into the black hole until finally, there is a point of no return. God's grace is more powerful than sin but a person has to want to change and follow Christ.

It may take a long time to exit the black hole and cross the event horizon that leads one out of the black hole. The problem is that in the black hole, time slows down because of sin.

If you want to find out the procedure to get out of the black hole or financial difficulties, let us turn to God's word. Paul, in 1 Corinthians, gives a step by step plan to move away from sin and self-serving ways.

"Now about the collection for God's people: Do what I told the Galatian church to do. On the first day of every week, each one of you should set aside a sum of money in keeping with his income, saving it up, so that when I come no collections will have to be made. Then, when I arrive, I will give letters of introductions to the men you approve and send them with your gift to Jerusalem. It seems advisable for me to go also, they will accompany me (1 Corinthians 16: 1-4).

This power-packed Scripture focuses on the six Ps:

- PURPOSE -- God's people
- PLACE – Your local Home Church or Place of Worship
- PRIORITY – First day of the week

- PARTICIPANT – Everyone
- PROPORTION – To your income
- PROTECTION -- God and oversees of the church

Just a word about the overseers of the church. Paul's purpose in this instruction was to give the first church a reminder to give gifts to the leadership who have its oversight—"the men you approve (1 Corinthians 16: 4)." They are responsible for the stewardship of the church and to provide an accurate and appropriate accounting of all the financial gifts. Therein lies protection from giving into a ministry that does not appropriately spend the money—otherwise known as a black hole.

The following are some summary points:

- God does not separate the gift from the giver.
- Cain's gift was careless and thoughtless compared to Cain's generous gift.
- The condition of Cain's heart is reflected in his face (anger).
- God's warning it is not too late. Cain has not fallen into the black hole as yet.
- How close are you to your black hole?

In the next chapter, I will discuss in further detail how to reach escape speed to get out of the black hole.

The Heart that Needs Saved

For we are God's workmanship, created in Christ Jesus to do good works, which God prepared in advance for us to do.

Ephesians 2: 10

When I was a young man growing up, I watched Tarzan every week on television. He always had the ability to swoop in and save someone from quicksand or danger. Don't we need someone like that today? Well, we do have someone even

> Sow a thought, and
> you reap an act;
> Sow an act, and you reap a habit;
> Sow a habit, and you
> reap a character;
> Sow a character, and
> you reap a destiny.
>
> Samuel Smiles

better than Tarzan, Superman, Wonder Woman, Batman or some other superhero. Jesus is our answer. We do not have to fear a black hole.

Once you have entered a black hole, you need to break free from its gravitational clutches. That can only be done when you have exuded enough force to overcome the drag. This is really a spiritual analogy.

If you are experiencing a financial black hole right now, you have options on getting out of it before there is a point of no return. You must start small. Remember, God entrusted you with all that you have and it is a sign of obedience when we give back to Him. You were made to do good works.

You may ask, should I pay my bills or give? Do both. Taking the first step, however small, is the beginning of the journey out of the black hole. There are many Scripture references about small gifts and this chapter will focus on several of them. "For we are God's workmanship, created in Christ Jesus to do good works, which God prepared in advance for us to do," states Ephesians 2: 10. This is one of the reasons listed in the introduction.

One of the great examples of a small gift is a young boy's gift of "five small barley loaves and two small fish," as it is reported in John 6: 9. Andrew adds, "But how far will they go among so many" as Jesus had just ministered to 5,000 men plus women and children.

Jesus said, "Have the people sit down" in verse 10. "Jesus then took the loaves, *gave thanks*, and distributed to those who were seated as much as they wanted. He did the same with the fish. When they all had enough to eat, he said to his disciples, 'Gather the pieces that are left over. Let nothing be wasted.' So they gathered them and filled twelve baskets with the pieces of the five barley loaves left by those who had eaten." John 6: 11-13.

Jesus is The Ultimate Bread of Life. He provides for you every day. You must trust Him that He has your best interest in His plans.

Also, giving thanks is an important part of getting out of the black hole. It propels you to see how God has blessed you with life, abilities, family members, and opportunities. After Jesus received from the small boy his gift of lunch, He multiplied it at least 5,000 times. He can do that for you too.

God may not immediately bless you for your giving. If you make it a habit of consistently giving and being thankful for such an opportunity, you will have a more blessed life by having internal peace knowing you are following God's design.

God wants us to be givers. In Mark 12, it explains how Jesus was teaching in the Temple and then he sat down opposite to where the offerings were being collected. Many rich people threw in large amounts, according to verse 41. "But a poor widow came and put in two very small copper coins, worth only a fraction of a penny," Mark 12: 42. Wikipedia states that it was valued at six minutes in a day's labor.
"Calling his disciples to Him, Jesus said, 'I tell you the truth, this poor widow has put more into the treasury than all the others,'" states Mark 12: 43-44.
"They all gave out of their wealth; but she, out of her poverty, put in everything—all she had to live on."

First, it is important to note that Jesus was watching who gave what. He saw the rich people throw in a portion, but He remarked about the widow who gave her all. A widow during Jesus' time was in a very difficult position. With no husband to take care of her, she may have had no property because it goes from male heir to male heir.

Sometimes you may feel you do not have much to offer. But Jesus is still watching today. He wants you to begin your efforts in giving and gradually increase as your income allows. The widow is an example to us today—Jesus wants us to give sacrificially to Him. What does giving sacrificially mean to you? Remember, … "but the Lord looks at the heart (1 Samuel 16: 7)."

Furthermore, the widow is not heard from again in the Bible. We do not know what happens to her. But I bet she is rejoicing in heaven because she stored up an eternal reward.

Sometimes we may not see here results for our sacrifice, good deeds, and works for furthering the kingdom here, but Jesus sees and does not let it go unnoticed. Her gift was small, but it was extravagant because it was all she had. You may feel that way too. That your gift is too small to make an impact. Let me assure you, Jesus is watching and approves of the steps you are taking to escape your black hole.

Throughout this book, I wanted to share different perspectives to legacy and giving. Mike Rollage works for a regional accounting firm for many years and has been associated with The Bible Chapel for over 31 years. He has been the finance team leader for the past 20 years and has seen changes in giving over the years.

"I believe that legacy is leaving something to be remembered by and we are leaving a part of ourselves for the future," he explains. "I have instilled in my children that we have a responsibility for giving back."

Over the years, Mike has supported his children and grandchildren with educational support, purchasing homes and providing a value system. "I would like to leave them zero dollars," he states. "I have sacrificed for them over many years."

Since seeing the church grow in the past 20 years, it has instituted new programs, new locations, and new missions. All this comes with a price though. "I believe my job is to help the elders and leaders of the church to understand that having a vision is great but we have to be good stewards of the resources God has given us to fund the vision. Remember, we are relying on giving trends to fund this," Mike says.

Teaching a class at the University of Pittsburgh, Mike would tell those who have been a financial black hole this advice. "Put a budget together and see what you are spending. Next, live on the budget. Perhaps you need to talk to credit counselors." He adds, "I follow my dad's advice, 'I earned and what I could afford, I spent.' I think people need to evaluate what are true needs."

Regarding giving, Mike suggests that people "prayerfully consider what to give. We should give responsibly after taking care of our family's basic needs (if you are in debt or struggling financially)."

He states that "giving is between them and God" and people should not give "because someone told them to do it."

He stated, "You have to persevere and there will be frustration but you have to balance that with the responsibility of good stewardship."

A member of The Bible Chapel's finance team for the past eight years, Peter Fleming believes, like Mike Rollage, that legacy is the impression you leave behind for your family and others. "I tell my two sons all that we have is a gift from God showing

> Saving, Investing and Giving Occur Best with Proper Discipline

His blessing and grace," he explains. "We should freely give it back first."

"When we first started to attend the church," Peter states, "the service was held in the Family Life Center and only girders were erected where the current sanctuary is now. I have also been fortunate to see the growth in the multi-sites from Robinson, to Washington and to Wilkinsburg and how there is a move of God in these communities."

In his role on the finance team, Peter looks for ways to structure or manage the vision from the pastors and elders. "Sometimes it is not easy and warning bells go off if we go off from the needs."

In addition, the church offers financial counseling to those who have experienced financial difficulties. "I would suggest they look at the lifestyle choices they are making and what items are beyond their control."

Another example in the Bible of generosity is Dorcas. She was also known as Tabitha, and was a Christian woman living in Joppa. She was known for her acts of charity, including the making of tunics and other garments for the poor. " ...All the widows stood around him (Peter), crying and showing him the robes and other clothing that Dorcas had made while she was still with them," reports Acts 9: 39.

The next few Scriptures are miraculous. Peter, with the power of the Holy Spirit, raises Dorcas from the dead. Maybe you feel dead and that there is no escape, but begin a good work, start to give at your church and see what God can do. He can push you through at escape speed.

According to Ron Kurtus in "Gravitational Escape Velocity for a Black Hole,"[6] a black hole occurs when a very massive sun or star that has collapsed on itself, such that its gravitational field is so strong than not even light can escape its pull. It is called a "black hole" because that is how it appears to telescopes.

"The equation for the gravitational escape velocity of a Black Hole uses the speed of light as the highest possible velocity for material trying to escape the star," states Kurtus. "The defining separation from the center of a Black Hole is called the event horizon or Schwarzschild radius and can be determined from the escape velocity equation."[7]

So there is a formula for escape from your financial black hole. Trust God to do His work. Transfer your faith and assets

---

6   Kurtus, Ron. "Gravitational Velocity for a Black Hole." School for Champions. March 8, 2011.

7   Kurtus, Ron. Ibid.

to Him and He will transform your life in unbelievable ways. Get ready to travel at warp speed now.

Matthew 10: 8, "Freely you have received, freely give." God wants us to be generous not an act but a response. Generous giving includes an obedient will, a joyful attitude and a compassionate heart.

THE OVERFLOWING HEART

*For where your treasure is, there your heart
will be also.*

Matthew 6: 21

Bill Harmon had a change of heart about seven years ago in 2007. He changed careers which changed his heart. He states, "At the beginning of your career, you are looking for something bigger than themselves and make a statement either through titles or paychecks that add to materialism."

He was "doing very well" but when "kids came along, I was thinking about what is important and looking to do things that I wanted to do," Bill explains.

Being the global vice president of human resources and global marketing, Bill enjoyed working with the people and the company where he was employed. A very high level position, Bill traveled extensively and his time was in demand.

"The company began changing and I went through a great transition to explore what I wanted to be involved with bringing my skills, talents and organizational abilities to build confidence and stability in an organization," states Bill.

He quickly accepted the executive director position at The Bible Chapel, McMurray, PA. "We prayerfully engaged in what we should be doing," said Bill as they examined spending habits and giving to needs of individuals and organizations.

"I wanted to give voice to people who were honoring God," said Bill, "and what stewardship represents."

Bill talks about Senior Pastor Ron Moore who has a gift of encouraging others. "If Ron sees someone who has the gift of teaching or craftsmanship, he earnestly works to engage them," he states. "Also, if someone has the gift of generosity, he encourages them to give to God's work. Giving is now highlighted as the act of worship it is. It is done with intentionality. It has been fun to watch," Bill observes.

Over the years, Bill and his wife, Lisa Anne, has put into action his thoughts on giving with their two daughters. "We tried to do with them growing up as to model behavior on the giving side and the serving side and Biblical solutions to problems."

They purchased three little buildings acting as piggy banks for their daughters to start them early on "stewardship and first fruits," Bill explains. "The first building was a bank for savings, the second for living expenses and the third was the church. There was a certain percentage if they received $10 they gave 10 cents to the bank and 15 cents to the church. It was interesting to watch as one was very disciplined on the savings and the other one was very disciplined in the giving."

"They learned early on that it is still God's money and His resources that He has given us," said Bill.

When traveling together, Bill usually observes the lottery signs. It begins a conversation with his daughters. "If you were to win $200 million in the Powerball what would you do with the money?" he asks. "Help others, have an eternal impact. They tell me what I want to hear. (Since they are both young adults) Pay down college debt and help Grandma and Grandpa."

Since a grandfather recently died, Bill asked his daughters how they remember him, which is his legacy. "They answered he was a gentle spirit and had a willingness to serve. He was a very successful marketing person but they did not focus on his career."

Legacy is a big term and can be daunting for some. "I used to think legacy was intertwined with philanthropy and for the uber wealthy such as Carnegie and Frick," said Bill. "I began to look at the behavioral sciences and what do you want to be remembered for and incorporate both. This is what I want my effort to be: benefit others after I am gone not only an inheritance for my family."

Obviously, helping others is a huge part of the church. It also includes financial issues. "If someone is having financial issues there can be other contributing issues which can be spiritual," says Bill.

"We try and handle short-term issues if someone needs some money for food, but we don't want to end there we want to help them develop discipline around stewardship," said

Bill. "We want them to say I am going to honor God with my commitments."

The church has a program where an individual or couple comes along beside someone in financial need and helps them with the basic understanding of finances such as developing a budget and living within their means.

"We need to protect our hearts and guard our hearts so we can truly help those in need," Bill states.

Another example of a changed heart is Greg Devore of McMurray, owner/operator of Mr. Handyman and an elder at The Bible Chapel. He said, "I don't believe in tithing." Of course, this created quite a stir. I was intrigued and I wanted to hear more about it.

"The New Testament Church is in the grace of God's plan," explains Greg. "All is given to us by God's grace and as we can, we should give back to Him and others. There is not a New Testament law on how much we should give."

He added, "We are created in God's image and we should not give reluctantly. We cannot out give God because we are adopted into His family."

Moreover, a pastor got up one Sunday and announced to his congregation: "I have good news and bad news. The good news is, we have enough money to pay for our new building program. The bad news is, it's still out there in your pockets." We don't want this to happen to us.

Randy Alcorn states in his book, The Treasure Principle: "The tithe is God's historical method to get us on the path of giving. In that sense, it can serve as a gateway to the joy of grace giving. It's unhealthy to view tithing as a place to stop, but it can be a good place to start."[8]

As you may recall in Chapter 1, Cain did not give an acceptable gift to God and he became cursed. Sin crouched at his door and he opened it. It is important to God to give the best we can.

"If we pay our debt to God first, then we will incur His blessing to help us pay our debts to men," states Mr. Alcorn. "But when we rob God to pay men, we rob ourselves of God's blessing. No wonder we don't have enough. It's a vicious cycle, and it takes obedient faith to break out of it."[9]

"There is preaching and teaching about who we are as children of God," states Greg. "We have rights, responsibilities and privileges as children of God. We are immigrants in this foreign land because heaven will be our eternal home but we want to live in both worlds at the same time with much consumption."

Paul tells us to be content in what we have been given. "I know what it is to be in need, and I know what it is to have plenty (Philippians 4: 12-13). I have learned the secret of being content in any and every situation, whether well fed or hungry, whether living in plenty or in want. I can do everything through Him who give me strength."

"You should be a good steward of what God has given you," explains Greg. "If you are in debt, you should give as

---

8   Alcorn, Randy. The Treasure Principle. Multnomah Books, Colorado Springs, CO, 2001. P. 64.

9   Alcorn. P. 66.

part of your worship to God. There is an obligation to meet your family's needs but remember you are doing God's work."

Greg added, "If you are working a minimum wage job, 10 percent may be a difficult stretch for you. You may need to give a smaller amount until your finances are straightened out. On the other hand, if a married couple is earning $100,000 a year and giving 10 percent that can be rather easily done. God knows the heart."

Paul speaks of the Macedonian church, "Out of the most severe trial, their overflowing joy and their extreme poverty welled up in rich generosity. For I testify that they gave as much as they were able and even beyond their ability. Entirely on their own (2 Corinthians 8: 2-3)." Sometimes you should give sacrificially, according to Steven J. Cole.[10]

"The church today, which is made up of individuals, is to be led by the Holy Spirit," states Greg. "Resorting to the law (10 percent tithe) limits what we are capable of accomplishing. Jesus always held the law to a higher standard. This was to demonstrate the fact that it is impossible for man to keep it."

I am not saying this will be easy. Any new habit you start or break takes a while to adjust, but it is worth it. The tithe is a benchmark we should strive to obtain if we have not reached it. But don't let it become a law issue.

Giving is a matter of the heart—let yours be full of abundance. Sometimes it may be scary to be generous. You may feel God tugging at your heart to be financially supportive of a

[10] Cole, Steven J. "Why You Should Not Tithe (Selected Scriptures)," God, Money and You series on Bible.org. P. 5.

neighbor or stranger. As stated before, God owns everything—we cannot out give Him. He will provide. Charles Ryrie states, "I would suggest that he give 9 or 11 percent just to keep out of the 10 percent rut. A person who is giving 9 or 11 percent will find himself much more sensitive to the Lord's changing his proportion than if he were giving 10 percent."[11]

"Out of the abundance of what Christ did for us, John 3: 16, should now compel us through the Spirit to do for others—'this is how we know what love is: Jesus Christ laid down His life for us. And we ought to lay down our lives for our brothers (1 John 3: 16),'" says Greg.

The Scripture, Luke 16: 10-13, really says it all—what are you trusting in? Money or God? You cannot do both. Choose today and make a difference in the life of your church. First fruits should go to your local, Bible-believing, Christ-centered church. This is where you are spiritually fed on a weekly basis. You can support worthy ministries if you evaluate their standards of operation and how they spend their money as you feel led by the Lord.

Giving can be really exciting. You are part of something greater than yourself and you've helping further the kingdom of God. According to www.livingonadime.com, its Sept. 23, 2011 edition, the average Christian spends 98 percent of their money on themselves and only 2 percent on God. Do you expect 100 percent from God? Sometimes I do. Do you need to share more of the resources He gave you?

---

[11]   Ryrie, Charles C. Balancing the Christian Life. Moody Bible Institute, Chicago, IL. P. 92.

> WHOEVER CAN BE TRUSTED
> WITH VERY LITTLE CAN ALSO
> BE TRUSTED WITH MUCH,
> AND WHOEVER IS DISHONEST
> WITH VERY LITTLE WILL ALSO
> BE DISHONEST WITH MUCH.
> SO IF YOU HAVE NOT BEEN
> TRUSTWORTHY IN HANDLING
> WORLDLY WEALTH, WHO WILL
> TRUST YOU WITH TRUE RICHES?
> AND IF YOU HAVE NOT BEEN
> TRUSTWORTHY WITH SOMEONE
> ELSE'S PROPERTY, WHO WILL
> GIVE YOU PROPERTY OF YOUR
> OWN? NO SERVANT CAN SERVE
> TWO MASTERS. EITHER HE
> WILL HATE THE ONE AND LOVE
> THE OTHER, OR HE WILL BE
> DEVOTED TO THE ONE AND
> DESPISE THE OTHER. YOU CANNOT
> SERVE GOD AND MONEY.
>
> LUKE 16: 10-13

You should always pray about your giving to God. He will not leave you without direction. During the early 1800s, John Wesley established the Methodist faith in America. He traveled by horseback to churches preaching wherever he could. He frequently preached on "get all you can, save all you can, and give all you can."[12] This came after a hard lesson he learned. Greg shared that Mr. Wesley used to smoke expensive cigars and lived an extravagant lifestyle. However, one day he saw his chambermaid had no coat and he wanted to buy her one. He did not have the money available to do it and he decided to change his ways. He began to limit his expenses so he would have more money to give away. You may have to change some of your ways as well.

---

[12]   Cole, Steven J., ibid. P. 6.

Biblical Guidelines for Giving

1.	Give as Exemplified by Jesus Christ	2 Corinthians 8: 9
2.	Give Systematically	1 Corinthians 16: 2
3.	Give Sacrificially	2 Corinthians 8: 2
4.	Give as a Privilege	2 Corinthians 8: 4
5.	Give with the Assurance that it is God's Will	2 Corinthians 8: 5
6.	Give as an Overflow of Love	2 Corinthians 8: 8
7.	Give as a Commitment	2 Corinthians 8: 11
8.	Give Proportionally	2 Corinthians 8: 12-15
9.	Give Generously	2 Cor. 9: 6-15, 2 Cor. 8: 7
10.	Give Willingly	2 Corinthians 9: 7
11.	Give Cheerfully	2 Corinthians 9: 7
12.	Give to the Glory of God	2 Corinthians 9: 12-13
13.	Give Because of God's Gift	2 Corinthians 9: 14-15
14.	Give Anonymously	Matthew 6: 2-4
15.	Give Without Ulterior Motives	1 Chronicles 29: 14-17

"All the believers were together and had everything in common. Selling their possessions and goods, they gave to anyone as he had need. Every day they continued to meet together in the temple courts. They broke bread in their homes and ate together with glad and sincere hearts praising God and enjoying the favor of all the people (Acts 2:44-47)."

This Scripture prepares us for the next chapter. These people shared from their heart and distributed to those in need.

A GENEROUS HEART

*But just as you excel in everything—in
faith, in speech, in knowledge, in complete
earnestness and in your love for us—see that
you also excel in this grace of giving. For
we know the grace of our Lord Jesus Christ,
that though he was rich, yet for your sakes
he became poor, so that you through his
poverty might become rich.*

2 Corinthians 8: 7, 9

I pray you are getting a hunger and thirst for giving. It really
can happen. You can really excel in giving through the help of
Jesus! A story of generosity
occurs when Jesus was
invited to have dinner at a
Pharisee's home, according to

> See that you also excel in
> this grace of giving.

Luke 7. It goes on to state that a woman who lived a life of sin and came to the dinner—she was an uninvited guest. She brought with her an alabaster jar of perfume.

At the time of Jesus, it was the custom to have someone wash the guests' feet, commonly a servant. It was also a custom to give kisses on the cheek as a welcome greeting. When Jesus entered the Pharisee's home, neither courtesy was extended to Him, according to the Scripture. Also, it was not uncommon to kiss people's feet as a symbol of humility, especially to a rabbi.

"She stood behind him at his feet weeping, she began to wet his feet with her tears," said Luke 7: 38. "Then she wiped them with her hair, kissed them and poured perfume on them."

I think it took a lot of tears to clean someone's feet who has been walking all over the countryside in sandals. Can you imagine it? What a humble, extravagant gift. She was not invited, women were not considered equals to men during that time, and perfume was an expensive offering.

The dowry was the item a bride brought to the wedding for her new husband. An

> All gifts are significant.

alabaster jar of perfume had to be an expensive item—maybe considered for a dowry. This woman willingly gave to Jesus her future.

It really is a mind-boggling gift even in today's standards of generosity.

"Therefore, I tell you, her many sins have been forgiven—for she loved much. But he who has been forgiven little loves little," as it states in Luke 7: 47. How much do you love the Lord? Can it be measured?

One thing that stands out about this Scripture is that the woman is not named nor does she utter a word, according to Bob Deffinbaugh, but her worship is lavish and true.[13] It was not easily hindered, it only focused on Jesus, she did not focus on receiving anything, and she was emotional. That is true worship. Jesus then tells her she is forgiven so she can love much.

Her life was truly transformed after she met Jesus. "Giving of money and things is a manifestation and responsibility of a truly spiritual life," said Charles C. Ryrie.[14]

Another example of generosity from individuals in the Bible who were influenced by Jesus was Zacchaeus. A short man, Zacchaeus climbed a tree when he heard Jesus was coming to his town. When Jesus saw him in the tree, he told him to come down and that He was going to eat at his home today.

"But Zacchaeus stood up and said to the Lord, 'Look, Lord! Here and now I give half my possessions to the poor, and if I have cheated anybody out of anything, I will pay back four times the amount.' Jesus said to him, 'Today salvation has come to this house, because this man, too, is a son of Abraham. For the Son of Man came to seek and to save what was lost (Luke 19: 8-9).'"

As you probably know, tax collectors were hated people during the time of Christ. Many of them took advantage of people and took too much compensation when they could. Jesus

---

[13] Deffinbaugh, Bob. "Wordless Worship of an Unnamed Woman," Bible. org. June 22, 2004

[14] Ryrie, Charles C. Balancing the Christian Life. Moody Bible Institute, Chicago, IL. P. 88.

changed Zacchaeus' heart in less than one day! He started to give away money almost immediately. How will you respond to God's unchanging love?

> Remember, God gave everything to you—money, a car, a home, plus a family and the ability to make money. I have been talking about finances in this book, but God really owns it all. Abraham was prepared to give his future back to the Lord.

In Genesis 22, it states that God tested Abraham. "Take your son, your only son, Isaac, whom you love, and go to the region of Moriah. Sacrifice him there as a burnt offering on one of the mountains I will tell you about (verse 2)."

Burnt offerings started in Genesis when Noah sacrificed animals after the flood waters receded. In Leviticus, it talks of "if the offering is a burnt offering from the herd, he is to offer a male without defect (1: 3)."

Abraham obeyed God quickly. The next morning, he got up and saddled his donkey. He took only two of his many servants and his son, Isaac. He cut the wood for the offering—can you imagine? They traveled three days to get to their journey. When Abraham saw where they were to go, he told his servants to stay with the animals. He and Isaac went on.

Isaac questioned Abraham by saying they had the wood and the fire but no lamb. Abraham said, "God himself will provide the lamb for the burnt offering, my son (Genesis 22: 8)."

Abraham took his son, bound him and placed him on the altar. He was ready to sacrifice his son as on offering to God. But the Lord intervened, "Do not lay a hand on the boy. Do not do anything to him. Now I know that you fear God, because you have not withheld from me your son, your only son (Genesis 22: 12)."

The Scripture does not say what Isaac thought of this, but Abraham was willing to give up his hope for the future. Genealogy is such an important issue to the Jewish people. Abraham needed a son to carry on his name, inherit all his riches and fulfill God's promises for his life.

This example was not necessarily financial, but it had financial implications. Abraham was willing to give what was so

> Giving is the antidote for materialism.

important to him. He recognized his need for God surpassed everything even his son.

God said "you shall have no other gods before me (Exodus 20: 2)." Abraham gave to Melchizedek his tithe and he was willing to give his son so nothing would be ahead of God.

Rylie added, "We give because He gave, not because we have to; we give because we love Him, and we show that love most concretely in this way. If in turn God blesses us materially, we praise Him; if not, we still praise Him. This is grace giving, and this is the proof of our love for God."[15]

---

[15] Ryrie, Charles C. <u>Balancing the Christian Life</u>. Moody Bible Institute, Chicago, IL. P. 92.

It reminds me of the great old hymn by Elvina M. Hall in 1865, "Jesus Paid it All."

I hear the Savior say,
"Thy strength indeed is small;
Child of weakness, watch and pray,
Find in Me thine all in all."

Refrain:
Jesus paid it all,
All to Him I owe;
Sin had left a crimson stain,
He washed it white as snow.
For nothing good have I
Whereby Thy grace to claim;
I'll wash my garments white
In the blood of Calv'ry's Lamb.
And now complete in Him,
My robe, His righteousness,
Close sheltered 'neath His side,
I am divinely blest.
Lord, now indeed I find
Thy pow'r, and Thine alone,
Can change the leper's spots
And melt the heart of stone.
When from my dying bed
My ransomed soul shall rise,
"Jesus died my soul to save,"
Shall rend the vaulted skies.

And when before the throne
I stand in Him complete,
I'll lay my trophies down,
All down at Jesus' feet.

AN OBEDIENT HEART

*And they send unto him certain of the
Pharisees and of the Herodians, to catch him
in his words. And when they were come, they
say unto him, Master, we know that thou
art true, and carest for no man: for thou
regardest not the person of men, but teachest
the way of God in truth: Is it lawful to give
tribute to Caesar, or not? Shall we give, or
shall we not give? But he, knowing their
hypocrisy, said unto them, why tempt ye me?
Bring me a penny, that I may see it. And they
brought it. And he saith unto them, whose is
this image and superscription? And they said
unto him, Caesar's. And Jesus answering
said unto them, render to Caesar the things
that are Caesar's, and to God the things that
are God's. And they marvelled at him.
Mark 12: 13-17 (King James Version)*

Before we start this chapter, I want to make a couple of things very clear. In the above Scriptures, Jesus reminds us to render unto Caesar what is Caesar's and to God the things that are God's. My wholehearted recommendations are:

- Pay your taxes.
- Pay your taxes in full.
- Pay your taxes on time.
- Pay all of the taxes you are required to pay.
- Don't pay any more than you have to!

Now that is out of the way, let us talk about good stewardship. A Christian steward is a person who is trusted with a life redeemed by Christ. There are five key principles of stewardship.

1. God alone is the sole and sovereign owner of all things.
   - He owns all creation and all that it encompasses. "To the Lord your God belongs the heavens, even the highest heavens, the earth and everything in it." Deuteronomy 10: 14.
   - He owns the body and spirit (life) of the Christian. "Do you not know that your body is a temple of the Holy Spirit, who is in you, whom you have received from God? You are not your own; you were bought at a price. Therefore honor God with your body." 1 Corinthians 6: 19-20.
   - God owns all of the Christian's resources. "For from Him and through Him and to Him are all things. To

Him be the glory forever! Amen" (Romans 11: 36) and "for the earth is the Lord's and everything in it." 1 Corinthians 10: 26.

2. The Christian is a steward of what God has given.
   * I must be a good steward of my life. "Therefore, I urge you, brothers, in view of God's mercy, to offer your bodies as living sacrifices, holy and pleasing to God – this is your spiritual act of worship." Romans 12: 1.
   * I must be a good steward of my time. "As long as it is day, we must do the work of Him who sent Me. Night is coming, when no one can work." John 9: 4.
   * I must be a good steward of my talents and abilities. "Each one should use whatever gift he has received to serve others, faithfully administering God's grace in its various forms." 1 Peter 4: 10.
   * I must be a good steward of my resources and possessions. "For if the willingness is there, the gift is acceptable according to what one has, not according to what he does not have." 2 Corinthians 8: 12.

3. Christian stewardship requires personal commitment.
   * I must commit to the Kingdom of God first and foremost. "But seek first His kingdom and His righteousness, and all these things will be given to you as well." Matthew 6: 33.

- I must commit to practical planning which facilitates godly living. "But I am sending the brothers in order that our boasting about you in this matter should not prove hollow, but that you may be ready, as I said you would be. For if any Macedonians come with me and find you unprepared, we—not to say anything about you—would be ashamed of having been so confident. So I thought it necessary to urge the brothers to visit you in advance and finish the arrangements for the generous gift you had promised. Then it will be ready as a generous gift, not as one grudgingly given." 2 Corinthians 9: 3-5.

4. God expects His sovereign ownership to be cheerfully acknowledged by presenting our life's gifts to Him.
   - Giving is a heart issue. "Each man should give what he has decided in his heart to give; not reluctantly or under compulsion, for God loves a cheerful giver." 2 Corinthians 9: 7.
   - Giving is an act of worship. "And whatever you do, whether in word or deed, do it all in the name of the Lord Jesus, giving thanks to God the Father through Him. Colossians 3: 17.
   - God holds each Christian accountable for what has been entrusted to Him.
   - "Therefore judge nothing before the appointed time; wait until the Lord comes. He will bring to

light what is hidden in darkness and will expose the motives of men's hearts. At that time each will receive his praise from God." 1 Corinthians 4: 5.

- For we must all appear before the judgment seat of Christ, that each one may receive what is due him for the things done while in the body, whether good or bad." 2 Corinthians 5: 10.

You may have seen throughout the book up to this point, that there is a tapestry being woven. Finances and your attitude towards giving impacts your entire life. God has given us many treasures, including a spouse, perhaps, children, property, and income.

Everything, yes everything we have is a gift from Him. He provides for us daily and has given us spiritual gifts. Yet with all this comes a great responsibility to manage these gifts well—time, money, talents, and even our family—in a way that honors God. We are called to be like Him and to be godly in our character.

Dave Stombaugh believes that legacy is "how they remember you after you're gone and that you continue after because of the impression you leave on people." Dave has been an accountant for many years and has served on the finance team at our church for the past 15 years.

Regarding his sons, Dave has valued that "they saw me giving and that it was part of life. I give every week and I set an example for them. I tell them you need to give but I also think that actions speak louder than words."

He added, "I believe it is important to give back to God for what He has given you."

Addressing those who have gotten into debt or a financial black hole, Dave offers this advice. "Live within your means. You do not need to buy the best of everything—home, car, clothes. It is important to help others and to not outlive your means."

"It is important to have a game plan to get out of credit card debt," explains Dave, "then the debt of a mortgage. You should have goals that are manageable and not outliving your means which would create problems that backfire."

Also, Dave addresses the growth of the church. "God has blessed our church with people sacrificially giving and that the church has not overextended itself to build it up. The interest rates have been low and we have manageable payments. We have been able to pay a substantial amount back (ahead of schedule)."

He concluded, "The pastors and leadership pray about it (what needs to be done—vision). It is not done by chance but with a lot of thought. As people consider their giving, prayer should be a part of it. They should give after they have prayed about it and have a peace over an amount."

There are many excuses and fears for not giving. Many people today fear losing their wealth or outliving it. God knows how many days we have here on this earth and He alone can provide for us if we trust Him.

Christian stewardship is not just about money, and we must take this

> Giving is an act of worship.

role seriously. We are called to trust God, but can He trust us? That is the question. Moments of selfishness and irresponsibility can rise up against us later in a powerful way. But also, small generosities can turn into greater gifts.

No matter if our income is small or great, we have the responsibility to do what God requires of us and to take care of those we leave behind. According to Wikipedia, estate planning is the process of arranging and anticipating for the disposal of one's estate during his or her lifetime.

Generally, it is important to have a will and appropriate beneficiary titles in place, particularly when minor children are involved. This is part of your overall stewardship of God's gifting to you. You need to have a will in place that directs your assets to your spouse, children, church, or other organizations, otherwise the state steps in and takes percentages of the estate to divide it.

As you ponder how your lifetime assets need to be divided, these are some other documents that you may need:

- If you have significant assets, you may consider establishing a trust. You need to seek legal and tax planning help with that.
- Whether you have health issues today or not, you need to decide before you are incapacitated what types of measures you want taken to keep you alive.
- You may need a power of attorney if through an accident or illness, you can no longer perform financial tasks in your best interest.
- Determine what ways are most effective to transfer your property to your children. Some common examples are

living trusts and the establishment of guardians if the children are under age.

- It is very important on your financial documents that you have the correct beneficiaries named. Generally, a will does not necessarily overturn named beneficiaries. Please review your insurance and financial documents to see if they follow your intentions.

- Life insurance, based on your age, can be a great benefit for a spouse, children or an organization you would like to receive a benefit from your death.

- Try and understand the tax laws concerning your estate. You must stay current with the tax laws because they are constantly changing in this political environment. See a good estate planning expert for help in this area.

- While you are living and can make these decisions, it is best how you want to plan for your funeral expenses. Do you want to be cremated or buried, viewing or memorial service? Also, do you want to donate any organs or your body to science? It may not be a discussion you want to have with your loved ones, but it can make your passing easier since you shared your preferences.

- Along that same line, you need to think of the service: do you want flowers? Music? An expensive coffin? Reception afterwards? With these details ironed beforehand, you can spare your family during the emotional time of your passing.

- You must let someone know, where you keep your important documents. After you die, it is not time for a hunting game. In a secure area, keep your financial documents which should include: legal titles to real estate property and/or cars, your will, trusts, insurance policies, stocks, bonds, annuities, bank accounts, mutual fund accounts, retirement accounts, credit card information, and/or any other debts such as utilities, taxes, mortgages, etc.

It is a lot to think about and do. Don't get overwhelmed, take one step and that will lead to another. You have provided for your family throughout your life and you want the transfer of assets to go smooth as well. "The way of a fool seems right to him, but a wise man listens to advice," states Proverbs 12: 15.

You may need a team of individuals to help with the planning process. Of course, you should start with your spouse and children if appropriate. An attorney, financial planner, tax accountant, funeral director, and hopefully, the pastor at your church. He or she can direct on planning a bequest gift so that your generosity can keep on going.

Also, you may want to talk to organizations that you have supported during your lifetime and may want to plan for a gift in your estate plans. There are options on how you may want to set up a gift to a non-profit organization. A foundation or donor advised fund may be a solution for you.

This charitable tool has become popular over recent years. The donor-advised funds program provides a donor with a simple, more effective solution, and a more inexpensive way for individuals engaging in charitable giving. The donor may give cash or other assets to a bank, financial institution or a public charity to establish a fund. Many banks have a charitable trust department which may utilize donor-advised funds. Fidelity Investments provides the Fidelity Charitable Gift Fund that is a simple, efficient, and effective solution to help facilitate your "giving" initiatives. You can find out more about Fidelity at www.fidelity.com.

Also, most charities have access to individual donor-advised funds. Depending on the institution, one can start "giving" with a nominal amount from $1,000 to $5,000 in many cases. Talk with your CPA about the tax benefits as well.

The fund is designed around the wishes of the donor. Donors may decide to fund the project on an annual basis or may create a long-term endowment. Donors have control over where the money is gifted although some institutions may have differing rules on that concept. The organization that holds the fund takes care of all of its financial, tax and administrative management. Those types of details must be worked out with the organization.

A private foundation would be a more costly endeavor to establish as opposed to a donor-advised fund. For more information, talk to your financial planner, your church, or your favorite charity to discuss your personal objectives and your specific situation.

"Have I not commanded you? Be strong and courageous. Do not be terrified; do not be discouraged, for the Lord your God will be with you wherever you go," Joshua 1: 9.

You may feel terrified during this process and not understand it fully. That is okay and to be expected. Take your time until you understand. You have taken your role seriously in God's kingdom and want to provide for your family. Take these steps with prayer and thoughtfulness. Do not enter it lightly.

Remember, God wants us to be generous not as an act, but as a response. Generosity includes having an obedient will, joyful attitude and compassionate heart. "Heal the sick, raise the dead, cleanse those who have leprosy, drive out demons. Freely you have received, freely give (Matthew 10: 8)."

Finally, this is not an end all. Life changes and you enter new seasons. You need to review your documents every several years or when a change has occurred such as your daughter gets married, you have a new grandchild, your son gets into medical school, you have a health issue, etc.

I think you prefer to make your own decisions as opposed to the State. They may determine that your spouse must share the wealth with your children now and leave you a small sum to live on for the rest of their life.

This process does not have to be expensive. But you need to be thorough. Start today.

Do I Need or Have I Checklist:

☐ Do I need a will? Is my will up to date and current?
☐ Do I need a living trust?

- ☐ Do I need a pour over will?
- ☐ Do I need a power of attorney?
- ☐ Do I need a medical directive?
- ☐ Do I need a living will?
- ☐ Have I updated my beneficiary designations?
- ☐ Have I shared this information with the appropriate people at the appropriate time?
- ☐ Have I been a good steward during this planning process?

But godliness with contentment is great gain.
I Timothy 6: 6

See the appendix for more information.

TRANSFORMED HEARTS

In the same way, any of you who does not give up everything he has cannot be my disciple.

Luke 14: 33

Psalm 111

Praise the Lord. I will extol the Lord with all my heart in the council of the upright in the assembly.

Great are the works of the Lord; they are pondered by all who delight in them.

Glorious and majestic are His deeds, and His righteousness endures forever.

He has caused his wonders to be remembered; the Lord is gracious and compassionate.

> He provides food for those who fear Him; He remembers His covenant forever.
>
> He has shown His people the power of His works, giving them the lands of other nations.
>
> The works of His hands are faithful and just; all His precepts are trustworthy.
>
> They are steadfast for ever and ever, done in faithfulness and uprightness.
>
> He provides redemption for His people; He ordained His covenant forever—holy and awesome is His name.
>
> The fear of the Lord is the beginning of wisdom; all who follow his precepts have good understanding. To Him belongs eternal praise.

As we have discussed through this book, are you more like Cain or Abel? I hope by now you can more identify with more Abel characters. Salvation is free, but ministry does have a cost and there is a cost to being a disciple.

In Hebrews 11: 4, it states, "By faith Abel offered God a better sacrifice than Cain did. By faith he was commended as a righteous man when God spoke well of his offerings. And by faith he still speaks, even though he is dead."

1. Joshua

Joshua had a different calling than Abel. He was a mighty warrior who led the Israelites into the Promise Land. Along with Caleb, he saw the opportunity not the problem. God spoke to him in Joshua 1: 9, "Have I not commanded you? Be strong and courageous. Do not be terrified; do not be discouraged, for the Lord your God will be with you wherever you go."

We have that same promise! God, through the Holy Spirit, is with us at all times. We can pray to Him and worship Him whenever we want. We do not need a high priest to do it for us; we can approach the throne on our own.

In Scriptures, it never states that Joshua doubted his role. Moses wanted his brother Aaron to speak for him (Exodus 4). Joshua trained with Moses. He was one of the 12 spies to see the land; he fought in battles. He was a mighty man of God. You can believe God for knowing your God-given destiny and following through. Be strong and courageous. God has overcome.

2. Daniel

Daniel, a handsome, young royal from Jerusalem, was taken to Babylonia in captivity. But Scripture does not share that he complained about his total change in lifestyle. "But Daniel resolved not to defile himself with royal food and

> Dependence +
> Obedience =
> Pleasing God.
> (See Deut. 28)

wine (Daniel 1: 8). The chief official in charge of Daniel's food was scared but God showed favor to Daniel and he looked healthier than the other ones (Daniel 1: 15).

His name got changed, but he adapted to his lifestyle. Daniel picked his battles. He did not eat the rich food and get drunk. He interprets dreams but gives God the glory. He won't bow down to the king and God protects him in a lions' den. I am sure these were not easy changes for Daniel but he resolved to stay true to his God.

3. Joseph

Joseph is a complicated person. He tells his brothers, who were jealous of him anyway, that they would bow down to him (Genesis 37). His father, Jacob, made him a coat of many colors and this infuriated his siblings.

Eventually, the brothers take action against Joseph and throw him into a pit then sell him into slavery. He ends up in Potiphar's household but his wife wants Joseph in her bed. Day after day, it seems, she tries to seduce him. He resists but the wife lies to her husband. Joseph is sent to prison.

In prison, he finds favor again. He runs the prison. During his time in jail, he meets the king's cupbearer and baker. He interprets their dreams for them. They come true. Joseph asks the cupbearer to remember him, but he quickly forgets (Genesis 40).

Pharaoh begins to have dreams. The cupbearer now remembers his promise to Joseph. Joseph cleans himself up before going before Pharaoh. Joseph, through God's help, interprets the dreams. Pharaoh then appoints him second-in-command and the organizer for the seven years of plenty and the seven years of famine (Genesis 41).

Joseph's brothers are having a hard time trying to survive. The years of famine are affecting the whole region. Jacob sends his sons to Egypt for food. Joseph recognizes them. After several tests, Joseph reveals himself to them. They have bowed down before him. His dream came true!

He gets to see his father again. But when Jacob dies, the brothers are afraid Joseph will take vengeance. "But Joseph said to them, 'Don't be afraid. Am I in the place of God? You intended to harm me, but God intended it for good to accomplish what is now being done, the saving of many lives (Genesis 50: 19-20)."

Joseph forgave his brothers and offered them life-sustaining food. Do you have that kind of forgiveness and obedience to God? Are you Abel?

4. Abraham

Lot's uncle definitely was Abel to withstand various trials and at the end, he became a father to many nations. Through Isaac, Israel was established. "By faith Abraham, when called to go to a place he would later receive as his inheritance, obeyed and went, even though he did not know where he was going," Hebrews 11: 8.

Would you have the faith to start a journey, say in giving, without knowing where it would lead? God may surprise you.

"By faith Abraham, even though he was past age—and Sarah herself was barren—was enabled to become a father because he considered Him faithful who had made the promise," states Hebrews 11: 11-12. "And so from this one man, and he as good as dead, came descendants as numerous as the stars in the sky and as countless as the sands on the seashore."

Abraham's legacy is assured for his faithful belief in God to provide land and heirs to him. Can you believe God will take care of you also?

5. Mary

Talk about a woman of faith. Mary was a virgin from Nazareth betrothed to a man named Joseph. During the time between betrothal and marriage, an angel, Gabriel, appears to Mary and tells her startling news. "Greetings, you who are highly favored! The Lord is with you," Luke 1: 28. Mary was "greatly troubled" at his words but Gabriel responded, "Do not be afraid, Mary, you have found favor with God. You will be with child and give birth to a Son, and you are to give Him the name Jesus. He will be great and will be called the Son of the Most High. The Lord God will give Him the throne of His father David and He will reign over the house of Jacob forever; His kingdom will never end (Luke 1: 29-33)."

Mary asks a practical question, how will this be since I am a virgin? "The Holy Spirit will come upon you and the power of the Most High will overshadow you. So the Holy One to be born will be called the Son of God (Luke 1: 35)."

"'I am the Lord's servant,' Mary answered. 'May it be to me as you have said (Luke 1: 38).'"

Wow! What an incredible response for a young woman. Her life was turned upside down. She needed to start over. Are you willing to make a move even if everyone is against it? What would you do if God directed you in a miraculous way? Sometimes we may have to take an incredible leap of faith!

She ponders things in her heart as Jesus grows. What was she thinking? What was it like to be the mother of the Son of God? It must have been incredibly hard to watch her Son suffer as He did and die. But what did she feel on Resurrection Day? Her Son died for her as well.

Think about Mary's example and how it can impact your life.

6. Paul

Paul seemed to have a privileged life as a youth. Educated by Gamaliel, a noted Jewish scholar, Paul was born a Jew but also a Roman citizen. As he grew, he became a zealot for his Jewish beliefs and sought to eliminate the Christian faith. But on the road to Damascus, Paul meets Jesus and he becomes a converted follower of the Way.

The writer of most of the New Testament, Paul is considered the apostle to the Gentiles. He was severely persecuted for his beliefs and was killed for them. Questions to ponder: what transformation have I undergone? How else do I need to change? What am I willing to sacrifice?

7. Peter

Becoming the rock of the church, Peter was an unlikely candidate. A rough and tough fisherman called out by Jesus, his life was transformed by the Savior. Nothing is written about his childhood; it must have included hard, physical labor. He could be hot or cold.

The second person to walk on water, Peter became afraid after he took his eyes off Jesus (Matthew 14: 28). Jesus said he had little faith; but he was the only one who got out of the boat. Are you being comfortable sitting in a boat? Maybe you need to stretch your legs a bit and test your faith.

Joann Naser's Story

There is a time for everything, and a season for every activity under heaven: a time to be born and a time to die ... He has made everything beautiful in His time. He has also set eternity in the hearts of men; yet they cannot fathom what God has done from beginning to end.

Ecclesiastes 3: 1, 11

This is one of my favorite Scriptures. There is a time for everything—a special season. There have been some hard seasons in my life—some that have brought much pain, but some have brought much joy.

I (Joann) accepted Christ at the age of eight at a Billy Graham Crusade in Pittsburgh. I went down front with my sister, Sue. We were raised in the Presbyterian Church so I knew the Bible but did not have a personal relationship with Christ until the Crusade.

I got married later in life by some standards, but we knew almost from the start that it was serious. Jim and I got married on October 5, 1991 after dating less than one year. Sometimes you just know the thing to do. We were able to get married then because someone was going to be sent overseas for Operation Desert Storm and had to cancel their wedding arrangements at the Summit Inn and Jumonville Chapel.

Happily married for less than two years, we welcomed our son, Jonathan Bennett, into our world. He is a joy. Six years later, we welcomed his sister, Elizabeth Rose, into our world too. There was a season in between of miscarriages and pain. She represents hope and a future.

November 19, 2007 changed our lives forever. Jim, Liz, and two friends were going to basketball practice. Jim was the coach of the team. He was hit by a drunk driver and was killed instantly. Liz was critically injured and had to be life flighted to Children's Hospital. The other girls sustained injuries too.

That evening, Liz had to have emergency brain surgery. Traveling to the hospital, I was unable to reach Jim not knowing at the time the extent of the accident. Arriving at the hospital, emergency personnel told Jon and me that Jim had not made it. How horrifying.

Sometimes time slows. I recall the instant—I had a choice whether to trust God in this situation or walk away from Him forever. I remember it was a conscious decision that was not made lightly although rather quickly.

I decided to trust God. It has not been easy. Watching Liz in the intensive care unit of the hospital was extremely difficult. The surgery was a success but she was placed in a drug-induced coma for 10 days so that her brain would not swell. She was also the first child in the United States to be involved in a cooling program that reduced her body temperature.

A miracle did occur there. Two weeks after the accident, she walked out of Children's Hospital with no need for additional physical, speech or occupational therapy. Liz surprised the doctors.

When we arrived home, it seemed quieter. It takes a long time to heal physically and mentally as well as spiritually. I will never know why this happened during my life here on earth but God is still sovereign and He still loves me.

I was a stay-at-home mom when Jim was killed. Liz was eight and Jon was 14. I wanted to be there for my children. I was their only parent now. Slowly, I got back into the workforce with the help of my sister, Peg, extended family, friends, church and Mike and Cathie McCormick.

I was blessed after Jim's tragic accident how the community supported my family. Strangers donated food, supplies, and finances to help land us on our feet. We were overwhelmed many times.

Since I was blessed, I believed I needed to continue to give of my time, talents and resources. I volunteered at Liz's school when she returned to the classroom. It comforted her to know I was nearby. We all began volunteering as helpers to first and second graders at Sunday school classes at The Bible Chapel, McMurray, PA and now in the nursery. I believe in financially giving as well a significant portion of our income.

God showed Himself faithful many times. He has not forsaken me or my children. I continue to praise His Name.

All these people did extraordinary things with God's help. He stretched them beyond their comfort zone. In the area of giving, are you willing for God to stretch you? Will you submit yourself to His authority and let Him take over your finances? Remember, He owns it all. Come on with me—let's step out of the boat into some uncharted waters. It should be quite an adventure.

> The Bible is not so much for information but transformation. "Do not conform any longer to the pattern of this world, but be transformed by the renewing of your mind." Romans 12: 2

A HEART AFTER GOD

Now He who supplies seed to the sower and bread for food will also supply and increase your store of seed and will enlarge the harvest of your righteousness. You will be made rich in every way so that you can be generous on every occasion, and through us your generosity will result in thanksgiving to God.

2 Corinthians 9: 10-11

Legacy. It is such a powerful word. What do you want your legacy to be? He really can take care of us. Don't you want to hear the Lord say, "Well done, good and faithful servant" to you (Matthew 25: 21)? I certainly do. There are some actions we can take to ensure a positive legacy to our family, friends, churches, and organizations we support.

First, let us look at the parable of talents in Matthew and glean some interesting ideas.

Again, it will be like a man going on a journey, who called his servants and entrusted his property to them. To one he gave five talents of money, to another two talents, and to another one talent, each according to his ability. Then he went on his journey. The man who received the five talents went at once and put his money to work and gained five more. So also, the one with two talents gained two more. But the man who had received the one talent went off, dug a hole in the ground and hid his master's money. After a long time the master of those servants returned and settled accounts with them.

The man who had received the five talents brought the other five. 'Master,' he said, 'you entrusted me with five talents. See I have gained five more.' His master replied, "Well done, good and faithful servant! You have been faithful with a few things; I will put you in charge of many things. Come and share your master's happiness!"

The man with two talents also came. 'Master,' he said, 'you have entrusted me with two talents; see, I have gathered two more.' His master replied, "Well done, good and faithful servant! You have been faithful with a few things; I will put you in charge of many things. Come and share your master's happiness!"

Then the man who had received the one talent came. 'Master,' he said, 'I knew that you are a hard man, harvesting where I have not sown and gathering where you have not scattered seed. So I was afraid and went out and hid your talent in the ground. See, here is what belongs to you.' His master replied, "You wicked, lazy servant! So you knew that I harvest where I have not sown and gather where I have not scattered seed? Well then, you should have put my money on deposit with the bankers, so that when I returned I would have received it back with interest. Take the talent from him and give it to the one who has the ten talents. For everyone who has will be given more, and he will have abundance. Whoever does not have, even what he has will be taken from him. And throw that worthless servant outside, into the darkness, where there will be weeping and gnashing of teeth."

Matthew 25: 14-30

So much in these few Scriptures. The allegory is that Jesus is the master. He has given us all talents and what do we choose to do with them? This parable puts people into two categories: do you do something with what you are given or do you bury it?

75

Think of your talents right now. Is there anything you are burying and not realizing its full potential? Do you like to sing, write, lead or volunteer at an institution? The exact same thing can be said about giving. As the man with the one talent said he was afraid of the Master. The "chief inhibitor to generosity isn't greed; it's fear," states Jeff Manion.[16]

Also, a talent (from Ancient Greek τάλαντον, *talanton* 'scale, balance') was a unit of weight of about 80 pounds (36 kg) and when used for money, it was the value of that weight of silver, according to Wikipedia. As a unit of currency, it was worth about 6,000 denarii. Since a denarius was the usual payment for a day's labor, a talent was roughly the value of twenty years of work by an ordinary person.

By modern standards, the 2014 federal minimum wage is $7.25 per hour, which would amount to approximately $300,000 over 20 years, while at the median wage of $26,363, it would be a half-million dollars. The talent as used in the parable is the origin of the word "talent" meaning "gift or skill" as used in English and other languages.

Sometimes, "more than not having enough, many people fear not being enough," said Manion.[17] This goes back to your legacy. You can have an impactful life if you get over your fear of not having enough or not being enough. Perhaps you think that is easier said than done.

---

16 Manion, Jeff. "Developing a Culture of Contentment." Leadership Journal. Spring 2013. P. 25.

17 Manion, Jeff. Ibid.

I have had several challenges in my life that I will share with you now. When I spoke at the Evangelical Church Alliance International 2013 Conference, I shared a quote from Theodore Roosevelt III when he landed on Utah Beach instead of Normandy Beach, we are not where we should be, said Roosevelt, "but the war starts here."[18]

In September 2008, the financial service industry was crumbling including banks, huge stock market firms, bonds and real estate. Since I work in the industry as president and CEO of BenchMark Wealth Management, I felt the weight of the uncertainty.

I carried 100 percent of the overhead of my business but the revenues dropped to 30 percent. It was a real challenge. I remember looking out the window of my office and thinking about what I should do.

During that time, I thought of the son, Mark, that my wife, Cathie, and I lost to cancer at the age of five. Any parent can understand the devastating feeling of loss that would accompany such an event. We also had other young children at the time. My daughter, Allison, was seven at the time of Mark's death and my oldest son, Michael, was eight. We had to fight that battle with a positive belief that God would bring us through. "And we know that in all things God works for the good of those who

---

[18] Colonel James Van Fleet, the regimental commanding officer, said in an unpublished memoir quoted in Ambrose, Stephen E. (1994). *D-Day, June 6, 1944: the Climactic Battle of World War II*. Simon & Schuster. ISBN 978-0-671-67334-5. That it was he who ordered "'Go straight ahead,'... 'we've caught the enemy at a weak point, so let's take advantage of it.'" Roosevelt's code talker, though, confirmed that Roosevelt made the decision.

love Him, who have been called according to His purpose," states Romans 8: 28.

As a family, we chose to bring something good from this significant loss. Cathie started the GriefShare ministry at The Bible Chapel, our home church, for those who have experienced the loss of a child, parent, sibling or spouse. Cathie also started a Candle Lighters of Pittsburgh ministry in this area for helping families with children who have cancer.

I am an elder at The Bible Chapel for the last 20 years and have been very involved in their capital campaigns to raise funds for the purchase of property and the expansion of the facilities. Allison has become a radiation oncologist focusing on breast cancer in women. She has two of our six grandchildren.

Michael is the lead pastor of a large church. We are very blessed by them and they both have careers helping others in differing circumstances.

Paraphrasing from Teddy Roosevelt III, the future starts right now. Your legacy and what you leave behind can be reshaped. Some issues are not of your own making, but you still have to deal with them. Use what you have and do what you can do is sound advice to getting back on track.

As I looked out my window in 2008, I made a decision. I went home that night and came back to work the next day in my best suit and I worked harder. Later, my administrative assistant would tell me, she noticed a change in me and she began to work harder as well as the rest of the office.

It was not easy, but we made it through that challenging time. I thought when I first established the business over 15 years ago, that the first years would be the hardest. Each year, we face different challenges and must know how best to adapt to them.

Children know the difference when you say, "do as I say, not as I do." I know we are being hypocritical. Do what I do—live a life of integrity and be consistent in your behavior. God has been faithful to me and my family. He is trustworthy and restorative.

Remember, money is a medium of exchange. We pay money for the things we value. Sometimes we get our values mixed up. Out of the 38 parables Jesus preaches, 17 are about money. In the four Gospels, Matthew, Mark, Luke and John, there are 288 citations about money. (See appendix for a more complete listing).

There are over 500 prayer Scriptures that Jesus refers to but 2,000 regarding money and possessions. Fifteen percent of Jesus' preaching was about money.

In today's standards, 80 percent of divorces are attributed to money issues. Over 90 percent of all crimes committed are due to money or sex.

The other god in our life can be money. What will it buy for me? I believe "afford" is the worst word in the English language. Our decisions regarding the uses of money should not be about what we can afford, but money should be used according to God's will and good Christian stewardship. Self-worth is not net worth.

Jesus loves us and we cannot be separated from Him if we have accepted Him as our Savior. "Be joyful always; pray continually; give thanks in all circumstances, for this is God's will for you in Christ Jesus," states I Thessalonians 5: 16. These are action words!

"Have I not commanded you? Be strong and courageous. Do not be terrified; do not be discouraged, for the Lord your God will be with you wherever you go," says Joshua 1: 9. Isn't that a comfort? This Scripture applies to every area of your life—financial, spiritual, and relational.

Let it be your legacy that whatever you have, you live a life of contentment and that you are not afraid to be generous. "Giving money away is one of the most powerful, countercultural, counter-materialism things a person can do," said Manion. "And I hate to see people postpone it into oblivion."[19]

Do you think the money in your pocket is really God's? I certainly don't all the time, but really it is. Intellectually I know that it is God's money and that I am the manager. That is why I need to pray continually and have giving as an act of worship.

I should give with as an act of the joy that is in my heart. When I stand before God, and I hope to hear, "well done, good and faithful servant," but He

> To parents and grandparents: Give them enough to give them an edge in life but not enough to take the edge away.

will also ask for an account of what I did with what he gave me. It is a sobering thought. Do I trust God with what He gave me or do I hang onto it as it is the last thing I will see?

---

[19] Manion, Jeff. Ibid. P. 26.

I believe savers do not go to prison. They believe they have enough and are not tempted to steal or commit a crime. Your legacy speaks of how you lived your life. Let it be one of satisfaction, praising God for what He has blessed you with and rich in the knowledge He has taken care of you.

There are additional Scripture references in the appendix regarding possessions.

Epilogue – Bringing It All Together

If anyone teaches false doctrines and does not agree to the sound instruction of our Lord Jesus Christ and to godly teaching, he is conceited and understands nothing. He has an unhealthy interest in controversies and quarrels about words that result in envy, strife, malicious talk, evil suspicions and constant friction between men of corrupt mind, who have been robbed of the truth and who think that godliness is a means to financial gain. But godliness with contentment is great gain. For we brought nothing into the world, and we can take nothing out of it. But if we have food and clothing, we will be content with that. People who want to get rich fall into temptation and a trap and into many foolish and harmful

desires that plunge men into ruin and destruction. For the love of money is a root of all kinds of evil. Some people, eager for money, have wandered from the faith and pierced themselves with many griefs.

I Timothy 6: 3-10

I want to give you some Scriptures that talk about how you should live your life. With these Scriptures, you can learn to trust God, transfer your faith into Him and He will transform your life! If we follow God's Scriptures, we can avoid "many griefs."

Command those who are rich in this present world not to be arrogant nor to put their hope in wealth, which is so uncertain, but to put their hope in God, who richly provides us with everything for our enjoyment. Command them to do good, to be rich in good deeds, and to be generous and willing to share. In this way they will lay up treasure for themselves as a firm foundation for the coming age, so that they may take hold of the life that is truly life. Timothy, guard what has been entrusted to your care. Turn away from godless chatter and the opposing ideas of what is falsely called knowledge, which some have professed and in so doing have wandered from the faith. Grace be with you.

I Timothy 6: 17-21

You can put your name in where it says Timothy, _____, guard what has been entrusted to your care. Lay up treasures in heaven rather than here on earth, states this Scripture.

> And then He told them this parable: 'The ground of a certain rich man produced a good crop. He thought to himself, 'What shall I do? I have no place to store my crops.' Then he said, 'This is what I'll do. I will tear down my barns and build bigger ones, and there I will store all my grain and my goods.' And I'll say to myself, 'You have plenty of good things laid up for many years. Take life easy; eat, drink and be merry.' But God said to him, 'You fool! This very night your life will be demanded from you. Then who will get what you have prepared for yourself?' This is how it will be with anyone who stores up things for himself but is not rich toward God.
>
> Luke 12: 16-21

Life carries no guarantees. We do not know when God will call us home, like when it happened to my son at the age of five. Do not be so focused on bigger cars, houses, and things that you miss God's calling on your life. Let me be clear—God is not against wealth; He is against idols or anything that sets itself before Him. Let your way be clear.

Also, people fear higher medical costs and how it impacts their deductibles and out-of-pocket expenses. Today, there is a deep sense of family obligation and taking care financially for children and now grandchildren.

Feeling that tax burden and issues around estate planning concern many in higher tax brackets. In addition to all that, there is information overload on all fronts regarding giving and charitable organizations.

My advice to you is to slow down, talk to God, and let Him direct your path. "Trust in the Lord with all your heart and lean not on your own understanding; in all your ways acknowledge Him and He will make your paths straight (Proverbs 3: 5-6)."

Living with the fear of money will cause you to miss out on God's promises. You can trust Him. I and a lot of others are living proof you can.

It is really time now to transfer your faith in Jesus Christ and allow Him to direct your life—all aspects of it—financial, relational, spiritual. "Surely God is my salvation; I will trust and not be afraid. The Lord, the Lord is my strength and my song; He has become my salvation (Isaiah 12: 2)."

He has become my salvation. Has He become yours? This giving plan can only succeed if you submit yourself to His authority. What an exciting journey it is.

Finally, some closing thoughts.

- Spend less than you make.
- Live a simple life.
- Pay off your home.
- Give money away freely as God inspires.
- Model a lifestyle to others that is simple and attractive.

You can create a climate of contentment in your home. That does not mean that you lack ambition, initiative or vision. It does mean that you trust 1 Timothy 6: 6: "But godliness with contentment is great gain."

May you experience His great gain.

Who I Am in Christ[20]

I am accepted ...

John 1: 12	I am God's child.
John 15: 15	As a disciple, I am a friend of Jesus Christ.
Romans 5: 1	I have been justified.
I Corinthians 6: 17	I am united with the Lord, and I am one with Him in spirit.
I Corinthians 6: 19-20	I have been bought with a price and I belong to God.
I Corinthians 12: 27	I am a member of Christ's body.
Ephesians 1: 3-8	I have been chosen by God and adopted as His child.
Colossians 1: 13-14	I have been redeemed and forgiven of all my sins.
Colossians 2: 9-10	I am complete in Christ.
Hebrews 4: 14-16	I have direct access to the throne of grace through Jesus Christ.

---

[20] Anderson, Neil. Living Free in Christ. Regal Books, Ventura, CA. 1993

I am secure ...

Romans 8: 1-2	I am free from condemnation.
Romans 8: 28	I am assured that God works for my good in all circumstances.
Romans 8: 31-39	I am free from any condemnation brought against me and I cannot be separated from the love of God.
II Corinthians 1: 21-22	I have been established, anointed and sealed by God.
Colossians 3: 1-4	I am hidden with Christ in God.
Philippians 1: 6	I am confident that God will complete the good work He started in me.
Philippians 3: 20	I am a citizen of heaven.

I am significant ...

John 15: 5	I am a branch of Jesus Christ, the true vine, and a channel of His life.
John 15: 16	I have been chosen and appointed to bear fruit.
I Corinthians 3: 16	I am God's temple.
II Corinthians 5: 17-21	I am a minister of reconciliation for God.
Ephesians 2: 6	I am seated with Jesus Christ in the heavenly realm.
Ephesians 2: 10	I am God's workmanship.
Ephesians 3: 12	I may approach God with freedom and confidence.
Philippians 4: 13	I can do all things through Christ, who strengthens me.

APPENDIX

Planned Giving Glossary

Glossary of Estate Planning and Planned Giving Terms

Estate Planning is part of our spiritual responsibility for the assets God has entrusted to us. When we realize that everything we own actually belongs to God and we are simply His caretakers or stewards, we understand the importance of making sure that those assets are passed on in a way that honors God and furthers His kingdom.

Asset
Property to which a value can be assigned; the property owned by a person or organization.

Beneficiary
To give or leave something by Will or Trust, typically personal property, cash or other assets.

Bequest

To give or leave something by Will or Trust, typically personal property, cash or other assets.

Capital Gain Tax

A separate tax charged on the profit from the sale of an asset that was purchased at a lower price. For instance, if an individual purchases stock for $100, then sells that stock for $500, he or she will pay capital gain tax on the profit of $400. Capital gain tax rates are usually different than income tax rates.

Charitable Remainder Trust

A Trust created by a donor that makes payments to the individual(s) for life or a period of years. At the end of the Trust term, the remaining balance in the Trust is distributed to charity. The donor receives a charitable tax deduction at the time of the gift to the Trust.

Charitable Lead Trust

A Trust designed to reduce beneficiaries' taxable income by first donating a portion of the Trust's income to charity. Then, after a specified period of time, the remainder of the Trust is transferred to the beneficiaries who typically face lower taxes.

Children's Trust

A Trust generally established at death through a Will or Trust. This type of Trust often has "rules" for how and when Trust proceeds will be distributed to children. A typical Children's Trust will distribute as much money as necessary for the care, support and education of the children. Often, when the children reach a certain age, the balance of the Trust assets are distributed to them for their personal use.

Corporate Fiduciary
An institution that acts for the benefit of another. One example is a bank acting as Trustee.

Double Tax Asset
Many people have retirement assets such as an IRA or 401 (k). The withdrawal from these accounts is subject to income tax. If such an asset is left to loved ones, they too will pay income tax on the amounts they withdraw from the accounts. If the Estate is large enough that it is subject to Estate tax upon death, the retirement assets are used to satisfy charitable bequests, both income tax and Estate tax will be eliminated on these assets.

Estate Tax
A tax imposed at one's death on the transfer of property.

Executor (or Personal Representative)
The person named in the Will to manage one's Estate after death. This person will collect the property, pay any debt and distribute property or assets according to the Will.

Fiduciary
A person or institution legally responsible for the management, investment and distribution of funds. Examples include Trustees, executors and administrators.

Gift Annuity

A contract between a donor and a charity that provides the donor with guaranteed fixed payments for life. The donor receives a charitable deduction at the time of the funding the Gift Annuity, and the annual payment percentage is based on the donor's age at the time the gift is made. In addition, a portion of each payment is tax-free. Upon the death of the donor, the charity receives the balance of the annuity.

Gift Tax

Tax on gifts generally paid by the person making the gift rather than the recipient.

Guardian

An individual legally appointed to manage the rights and/or property of a person incapable of taking care of his or her own affairs.

Income in Respect of a Decedent

Income in Respect of a Decedent is income a decedent earned and was entitled to before death, but was not included in the decedent's gross income.

Intestate

A person who dies intestate has no Will, and the State then designates how their estate will be distributed.

Joint Ownership

The ownership of property by two or more people, often with right of survivorship. The survivor thus ends up owning the property outright upon the death of the other party.

Living Will

A living will is a document that allows a person to explain the type of medical treatment that they wish to receive in the event of a terminal illness where death is imminent. A Living Will often indicates when life support, hydration or nutrition may be removed. Laws governing Living Wills vary by state.

Marital Deduction

A deduction allowing for the unlimited transfer of any or all property from one spouse to the other, generally free of Estate and gift taxes.

Power of Attorney for Health Care

A document that authorizes another person (an advocate) to make health care decisions for an individual if he or she is incapable of making their own decisions.

Power of Attorney for Property

A document that authorizes a person (described as the agent) to conduct financial transactions for another individual. The agent's power can be restricted within the document. A Durable Power of Attorney for Property is valid even if the individual becomes incapacitated.

Probate

The probate process, with regard to a decedent's Estate, occurs when the court oversees the distribution of a decedent's assets.

Revocable Living Trust

An Estate Planning tool that provides for the convenient administration of the assets in an individual's Estate without the necessity of court supervision. When assets are transferred into a Revocable Living Trust (a process called "funding"), the trustee can manage the assets in the event of the individual's incapacity or death. This type of Trust is often used to avoid the probate court process and can also be used to provide ongoing management of assets after one's death. A Revocable Living Trust can be amended or revoked until such time as the individual is incapacitated or deceased.

Testamentary Trust

A trust that is created upon death by the terms of a person's Will.

Trustee

The individual or institution entrusted with the duty of managing property placed in the Trust. A "Co-Trustee" serves as a Trustee with another. A "contingent Trustee" becomes Trustee upon the occurrence of a specified future event.

Will

Often referred to as a "Last Will and Testament," a Will is a final statement of one's wishes regarding the assets in one's Estate. A Will does not eliminate the need for probate court intervention as many people mistakenly believe, but it gives the probate court direction as to how the assets should be distributed. In most states, a Will is the document used to name guardians of minor children.

Information from <u>www.barnabasfoundation.com</u>

POSSESSION PARABLES

Wise and foolish Builders	Matthew 7: 24-27
Sower and soils	Luke 8: 11-15
Hidden treasure	Matthew 13: 44
Valuable pearl	Matthew 13: 44
Unmerciful servant	Matthew 18: 23-24
Workers in the vineyard	Matthew 20: 1-16
Tenants	Matthew 21: 33-44
Faithful and wise servant	Matthew 24: 45-51
Talents	Matthew 25: 14-30
Moneylenders	Luke 7: 41-43
Good Samaritan	Luke 10: 30-37
Friend in need	Luke 11: 5-8
Rich fool	Luke 12: 16-21
Shrewd manager	Luke 16: 1-8, 13
Rich man and Lazarus	Luke 16: 19-31
Master and his servant	Luke 17: 7-10
Pharisee and the tax collector	Luke 18: 10-14